FOOTBALL SKILLS:

UNIQUE STEP-BY-STEP TRAINING TO HELP YOUNG SOCCER PLAYERS WIN

FOOTBALL SKILLS

ONE-TO-ONE TEACHING FOR THE YOUNG SOCCER PLAYER

Ralph Brammer

RIGHT WAY

Constable & Robinson Ltd
3 The Lanchesters
162 Fulham Palace Road
London W6 9ER
www.right-way.co.uk
www.constablerobinson.com

First published in the UK 2000

This edition published by Right Way, an imprint of Constable & Robinson,
2008.

A copy of the British Library Cataloguing in Publication Data is available
from the British Library

ISBN: 978-0-7160-2206-0

Printed and bound in the EU

1 3 5 7 9 10 8 6 4 2

Dedicated to all the youngsters who play football and to all the adults who help them. Special thanks to my partner Heather for her input and support, to Ryan Flannery for his role as the pupil and to Louis Julius for using his skills. Caring thoughts to my late wife Wendy and daughter Lisa: I'm sure they're looking down waiting to see a football star evolve from the book.

Acknowledgements to:

James Wilde for the lovely drawings.

My daughter Suzanne and sons Ray, Ryan and Mark.

Dave Thompson and Craig Roberts for their help.

John Billington for his initial help with photography.

CONTENTS

INTRODUCTION

Football (Soccer) has changed much over the years. This once friendly kick about is now a much sought after career.

Budding stars now begin football at the age of eight or nine, both in school and club matches, with thousands more competing in league games each year. All are eager to win titles or trophies and make their way to football fame.

Football now holds the key to large financial rewards, so parents and youngsters are keen to explore the road to success. Junior levels of football are also fun in themselves. Yet no matter what level of football you play, and regardless of possible financial gain, there is more purpose and pleasure if you play really well.

Many players of all age groups lack skill. Errors are made in kicking or controlling the ball. Faults often occur with technique, timing, and patience. These faults may give rise to frustration that often leads to aggression or bad habits.

How can a youngster play better? Just look closely at his skill, test his ability and know how to bring out the best. Soccer skills are vital, skills such as shooting, passing, ball control, heading. They are the essential foundation for success.

The purpose of the book is to show youngsters what to learn, and parents how to teach. The method is a unique plan using a one to one formula and step by step guide. It is a progressive route to build up confidence and all round skills. There is due emphasis on speed and timing, parents can analyse what their child is lacking in, and thus remedy any shortcomings.

The book does not attempt to cover such aspects as goalkeeping, team tactics, set moves, or rules of the game, but the final part gives good advice on playing in a team and the standards to set.

An Important Foundation

Lessons one to five are the basis. They highlight strengths and weaknesses. They are designed to correct bad habits and steady a youngster.

Lessons six to fifteen elaborate the fundamentals. They give variation to the basic techniques, foster quick thinking, and co-ordinate movement. They are designed to increase the youngster's skill, composure and confidence on the ball.

Part 2 of the book is a résumé and summary of what every coach and youngster need to know about The Game.

Fig. 1 The Game at its biggest!

How to Use the Book

Follow the lessons in sequence and from the beginning. This will set you on the correct path.

It doesn't matter if you can't get into a football team, or have only just started playing, whether you play in a team that always loses, or one that mostly wins.

You Can Improve Dramatically. How?

From one-to-one teaching lessons	GREAT
Gain confidence on the ball	SAFE
Discover balance and timing	WICKED
Learn to execute skills correctly	SPOT ON
Learn to execute skills in the correct sequence	OF COURSE
Learn to control and pass the ball with either foot	OOPS
Learn to shoot and hit the ball long using either foot	WOW
Head the ball correctly in attack or defence	EXCELLENT
Recognise your skills and how to use them	CLEVER
Use your new found talent on the field	COOL

Fig. 2 Gain confidence and show off your skills on the field.

What do I Need?
- ✓ A football. Well, you don't say.
- ✓ A playing field, garden or, if necessary, just a hard surface. Do not use your football too much on a hard surface or you may end up buying a new ball fairly quickly.
- ✓ A brick wall to practise against. Make sure you are not annoying the neighbours, or dare I say, 'using their wall'.
- ✓ A sensible person to teach you, practise with and look for good points or mistakes. Dad (or Mum) will do nicely. Later on, a competent person to pass the ball to you. But again, I'm sure Dad will be fine.

Fig. 3 Dad will do nicely.

The Ball
Good low cost leather balls are available in most sports shops.
The ball needs to be a standard size five, or smaller if the child
is young. The correct sizes for different ages are:

Ages 8 and under	Size 3
Age 9 to 14	Size 4
Ages 15 and over	Size 5

Do not pump the ball up too hard, just fairly firm. This is
particularly important for younger boys. An adult should be
able to indent the ball slightly with his thumb.

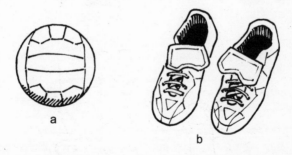

Fig. 4   a) The ball.
b) The boots.

Your Boots or Trainers
Your football boots or trainers need to be the correct size,
above all they must feel comfortable.

Right from the Start
On average you only have about three minutes' ball possession when playing a full game of football. Not a lot is it? So
get it right from the start.

Fig. 5   a) Stretching exercises! Cross legs, do not bend knees, try touching toes.
b) Open legs, bend one knee, lean sideways with other leg.
c) Arms out, slowly turn body from the waist.

Important for Teacher and Pupil: Warm Up First
Light jogging on the spot and some stretching exercises will do. Please make sure you warm up before any practising otherwise you could pull a muscle . . . OUCH! This would more than hinder your football for a while. If you are not sure what stretching exercises are, ask your P.E. Teacher. Fig. 5 shows some stretching exercises in the standing position. Exercise gently and slowly.

For clarity of expression we will from now on use the terms 'pupil' and 'teacher'.

TEACHER

The First Lessons
The first five lessons are basic but do not underestimate their value. All players must start on the right footing, and these

lessons may give more of an insight than you expect. So let's see how to perform at the simplest level.

It is sometimes difficult to get through to youngsters, or make them listen; as we all know, most kids think they know best. But, be patient and show the child correctly. Then if the child does well at each practice, he will be more confident, and look forward to the next one.

Do not spend too much time on each exercise, but be prepared to go back, try again and practise regularly. Read the whole section before you start each exercise and take note of the **bold text**, this highlights key aspects. You must, however, spend more time with the first lesson striking the ball. This will give the pupil a feel for many other skills and set him on the correct path.

PUPIL

A Side to Encourage

From an early age we all have a tendency to use one particular side of our body for particular things. We mostly use our right hand to throw a ball, write, comb our hair and so on. Or to stand on a chair we will always use our stronger foot first to balance. Well, in football these one-sided strengths or weaknesses are detrimental. Problems will occur from not being able to use either foot to strike the ball. This leads to an imbalance in the way you play your game. A 'one-footed' footballer suffers from serious limitations.

LESSON 1

BALANCE AND STRIKING THE BALL

PUPIL   Always strike the ball using the lace area of your boot. This will ensure you can shoot, hit long passes and, when experienced, score some real power drives. This method of striking the ball is **vital for you to learn** and is therefore thoroughly explained.

The first exercise is solely balance but will give you
- an insight into striking the ball
- a feel for the movement
- an idea of the action using either foot.

Don't skip these exercises, they will not take up much time.

Look at fig. 6a. Balance on your right leg with **knee slightly bent** and arms out. Lean forward and look down. Bring your other leg backward **bending your knee,** then forward as if you were kicking a ball. Practise slowly.

Now look at fig. 6b. **Point your toes downwards** and imagine kicking the ball **using the lace area of your boot. Keep your eyes on the spot where you think the ball would be**.

A steady balance is the key. Follow through with your kicking leg, which should end up straight, as in fig. 7a.

Next, try balancing on your right leg, then left leg. Imagine the ball is in place and let your hip swing naturally. Practise until you feel comfortable enough to attempt kicking the ball with the lace area of **either** foot.

Fig. 6 Imagine kicking the ball.

Fig. 7 a) A good follow-through.
b) And try the other foot.

First Learn to Strike a Ball

PUPIL Place your right kicking foot (lace area) up to the ball with **knee bent and toes pointing down**. Look at fig. 8a. Your eyes should be on the ball. Now turn your heel **very slightly inwards**. Fig. 8b shows the position exactly. You now have your kicking foot in the correct position to strike the ball. Your standing foot **should be alongside the ball** (about 10cm away) **pointing in the direction you want the ball to go**. Keep practising this position many times with your left and right foot.

Fig. 8 a) Correct position of contact.
b) Heel inward.

Preparing to Strike the Ball

PUPIL Take up the same position again. Now bend your knee and bring your foot away from the ball about 20cm, as in fig. 9a. Wait a second. Now with the lace area of your boot, gently strike the ball, as in fig, 9b. Practise this with your **left and right foot alternately. For the time being, always strike the ball with the centre of your foot and hit the middle part of the ball. This will enable you to direct the ball straight and low when it leaves your foot, as in fig. 10. Always keep your eye on the ball**.

a   b

Fig. 9   Striking the ball.

Now Strike the Ball Slightly More Firmly

PUPIL   Take up the same position but bring your leg and foot further back and execute the strike in one complete steady movement. But as your foot **nears** the ball **increase the speed of your foot** and strike the ball with a **quick smart tap**. The sequence is shown in fig. 11. Always look closely at the ball. As your foot nears the ball increase the speed of your foot. Feel the ball leaving the lace area of your foot. If your foot makes correct contact the ball will travel quite fast without much effort, so don't strike the ball hard.

Fig. 10   Ball travels straight and low.

Fig. 11   Hit it a bit harder.

You **must** use your right foot and then left foot and so on, especially at this stage.

| TEACHER | Tell the pupil, "take your time, eye on the ball, gentle strike" (strike meaning use the lace of your boot). Watch the pupil's performance whilst giving the orders, Mr Manager!

Hit the Target

| PUPIL | Place a target on the floor, or mark a point, 6–7 metres in front of you. Approach the ball from behind but slightly to one side and kick it to hit the target using your right foot and then your left, as shown in fig. 12. **Bend your knees and keep your eye on the ball. Use a steady leg action with a slightly quicker strike.** You may feel awkward striking the ball with your left and right foot. However, keep trying and you will get there. **Accuracy is the key at this stage, not whacking the ball!** Power comes later.

Fig. 12 Ready to walk and strike the ball.
Right foot strike.
Left foot strike.

TEACHER Remind the pupil, "**take your time, eye on the ball, gentle strike**". Tell the pupil to practise the approach sequence of striking the ball, but **stop his foot just as it is about to strike the ball**. This will enable both you and the pupil to see any faults. To ensure the pupil hits the middle part of the ball, remind him to "**fix your eyes on a point at the middle of the ball**". Looking at a central point on the ball will give a guiding effect.

A typical mishit results from the pupil:

- not keeping his eye on the ball
- not placing the non-kicking foot to the side of the ball
- not hitting the middle part of the ball.

More Right and Left Foot Accuracy

PUPIL Place two smaller targets 2–3 metres either side of the main target, as in fig. 13. Stand behind the ball and aim at these new targets. Practise the left foot then the right foot and so on.

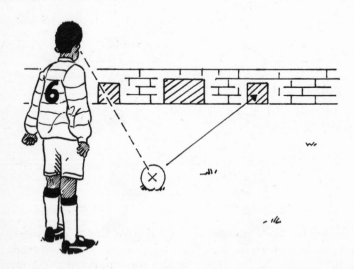

Fig. 13 Practise again with additional smaller targets.

TEACHER We now see a change from the last exercise to give the pupil a different feel for the ball. This is a useful test of timing and accuracy.

Stand facing the pupil. Now throw the ball gently (under arm) towards the pupil's right or left foot, allowing the ball to bounce once before reaching him. The pupil uses first his left then right foot and so on to strike the ball gently back to you. Remind the pupil, **"take your time, eye on the ball, gentle strike"** – again, striking with the lace area of the boot.

Fig. 14 Throw the ball directly onto the pupil's foot.

Now move closer to the pupil and **throw the ball directly onto his left or right foot**, as in fig. 14. The pupil should gently strike the ball back to you, **low into your arms**. Throw the ball accurately and you will find that this is a good test for the youngster.

Useful Practice on your Own

PUPIL Follow the sequence shown in fig. 15. Drop the ball in front of you, let it bounce once, then gently strike it against a wall. When the ball returns, let it bounce on the ground then, using the other foot, gently strike it back against the wall. **Use the lace area of your boot and keep the ball low. Use your right foot and then left foot and so on until you build up a continuous flow**. Keep a steady rhythm by **repositioning yourself quickly for the bounce**. If you can't keep the flow going, stop the ball and start again.

Fig. 15 Kicking the ball against a wall.

More Practice on Your Own – Strike the Ball Low and Get a Feel for the Action

PUPIL Stand 2–3 metres away from a wall. Place one foot **alongside** the ball then strike it against the wall, as in fig. 16. See if you can make the ball travel close to the ground and come back to you fairly accurately. Trap the ball using the inside of your foot and start again. Practise first with your **right** foot, then use your **left**. **Lean slightly forwards with your arms out for balance and keep your eye on the ball.** Next, you are going to strike the ball while it is moving:

● Strike the ball back and forth off the wall using only your **right** foot. You will need to **move quickly into a good**

Fig. 16 Strike the ball low with the right foot . . .

position to strike the returning ball. Hit the middle to top part of the ball to keep it low.

● Now try using only your left foot to strike the ball back and forth off the wall, as in fig. 17.

● Next, strike the ball back and forth off the wall using alternate feet.

Fig. 17 . . . and then the left foot. Move quickly to strike the returning ball.

LESSON 2

TRAPPING AND CONTROLLING THE BALL WITH YOUR FEET

We will return to striking techniques again, but for now let's move on to the second lesson: how to control the ball and produce the right effect. It is easier to control a ball on the ground than one in the air, however we don't want to make things too easy for you.

PUPIL The best way to control a ball at waist height or below is to use the inside of your foot. Judge where the ball will land and place your foot accordingly, or bring your foot up in the air. The ball should end up on the ground, in front of you.

Sounds easy? Then why do we see so many errors on a football pitch, especially at lower levels? **You must be in control of the ball – do not let the ball control you**. Do not chase after the ball frantically if you make a mistake. This is a waste of energy and only indicates the need to practise.

TEACHER Stand facing the pupil, 2–3 metres away from him. Throw the ball so it lands on the **inside** of the pupil's right foot, as shown in fig. 18. Now do the same with the left foot. Throw the ball low to the ground, varying up to waist height, and call out "**eye on the ball**".

PUPIL **Keep your eye on the ball and relax**. Bring your foot back at **the same speed as the ball** to cushion it at the

Fig. 18 If your foot remains rigid, the ball will bounce from it. Bring your foot back at the same speed as the ball to cushion it.

Fig. 19 Control a high ball by lifting your foot up and back to cushion the ball. The ball then drops to the ground.

moment of impact. If the action is correct, the ball will then drop near to your feet, as in fig. 19.

TEACHER Once the pupil has learnt this technique, steadily increase the distance between you. Walk backwards 50cm at a time and throw the ball again. But from now on, as soon as the pupil makes contact with the ball, call "**head up**". **The pupil needs to look up without delay** (see fig. 20). Tell the pupil to strike the ball back to you gently, using alternate feet. Tell him to "take your time, eye on the ball" and so on. Repeat this until you are 6–7 metres away from him.

Fig. 20   After contact with the ball, call "Head Up".

Build up to a Quicker Reaction with Steady Ball Control

TEACHER Always throw or kick the ball fairly accurately to the pupil. You may need to pass the ball along the ground if the pupil is young, but still tell him to bring his foot back to cushion the force of the ball.

Using the exercise above, face the pupil, 7–10 metres away from him. The pupil should turn his head and look either to the left or to the right (see fig. 21). Throw or kick the ball to the pupil and, at the same time, call "**control**". The pupil needs to respond quickly, look at the ball, move if necessary, and then control the ball using the inside of his foot. Afterwards, tell him, "**head up**" and then he should gently strike the ball back to you.

a   b

Fig. 21 The pupil waits for the teacher's command.

- Now do the same exercise, but first tell the pupil which foot to trap the ball with.
- Now do the same exercise again, but this time tell the pupil which side to turn to.

Useful Practice – Trapping the Ball on your Own

PUPIL   Drop the ball in front of you. Gently strike the ball
against a wall using your right foot, as in fig. 22. When the
ball bounces back, control it using the inside of your left foot,
as in fig. 23.

Fig. 22 Strike the ball with the right foot . . .

Now strike the ball with your left foot, trapping it with your
right, and so on.

Fig. 23 . . . and trap the ball with the left foot.

LESSON 3

BASIC AWARENESS

You will have more practice trapping the ball later on, but for now let's try something different.

It is very important for players to know what's going on around them. Imagine being in the centre of a football pitch, watching a game with fast action in the midfield area. This back and forth movement could make you dizzy, or send you reeling. A player will turn many times in a game, and so it is important to practise some circular movements. The following exercises will improve the pupil's perception and orientation, whilst at the same time increasing his confidence with the ball at his feet.

| PUPIL | Walk in an imaginary 8 – 10 metre diameter circle (see fig. 24c) with the ball at your feet. As in figs. 24a and 24b, keep your **head up, look ahead, left and right, only ever glancing at the ball briefly**. Use alternate feet to control the ball, keeping it close to you at all times. Now turn and walk the circle in the other direction.

Jogging the Circle
Jog the same circle with the ball but, halfway around, stop the ball by putting the sole of your boot on it, as in fig. 25a. Now turn quickly and take the ball the other way. Keep your **head up** and keep the ball close to you.

Practise this a few times and slowly build up speed without losing possession of the ball. **Do not run too fast** as this may make you dizzy.

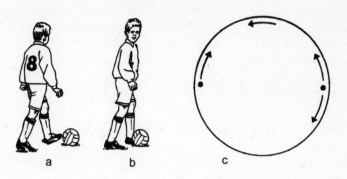

Fig. 24   a) Look ahead with the ball at your feet . . .
b) . . .look to the right and the left too.
c) Walk an 8–10m diameter circle.

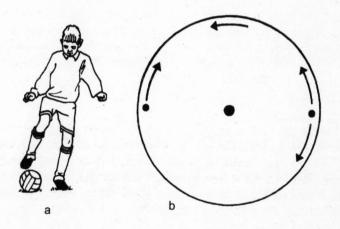

Fig. 25   a) Stop the ball with the sole of your boot.
b) The teacher stands at the centre of the circle. When he calls "turn", the pupil changes his direction and takes the ball the other way.

TEACHER   Look at fig. 25b. Stand in the middle of the imaginary circle. From time to time, reverse the direction that the pupil jogs by giving the command "**turn**". Now tell the pupil to stop the ball using alternate feet: give the commands "**left foot turn**" or "**right foot turn**". Call "**head up**" after each turn.

Be Aware of What's Going on Around you – Feel the Ball at your Feet

| PUPIL | Jog around the same circle again, but this time stop at each half of the circle. Face the centre of the circle, place one foot on top of the ball and pivot backwards in a small circle, as illustrated in figs. 26a and 26b. Use the sole of your boot to guide the ball around with you. For anticlockwise circles, use your left foot on the ball; for clockwise circles, use your right foot. After turning on the spot you should end up facing the centre of the larger circle again. **Keep your head up** whilst controlling the ball.

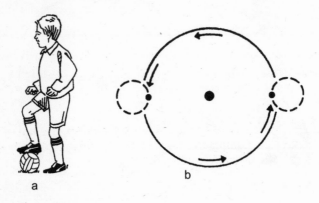

Fig. 26   a) The teacher calls "stop" . . .
b) . . .and the pupil rolls the ball backwards as he pivots in a small circle.

| TEACHER | Stand in the middle of the circle and give the command "**stop**". Now tell the pupil which foot to use to roll the ball.

Small Forward Circles

PUPIL   As before, jog the circle, in either direction, with the ball at your feet. At each half of the circle, take the ball in a small forward circle and continue on in the same direction as before (figs. 27a and 27b). Practise the small circles anticlockwise then clockwise. Control the ball using the **inside** of your feet. **Keep your head up and only glance at the ball now and again.**

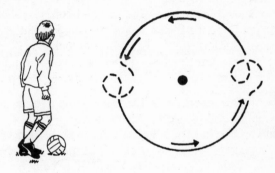

Fig. 27   The pupil takes the ball in a small forward circle, then continues in the same direction as before.

TEACHER   As the pupil reaches the half-way point of the circle, give the command "**small circle**" and indicate whether it is to be clockwise or anticlockwise.

LESSON 4

HEADING THE BALL

We will return to circle moves again but, for now, another lesson.

PUPIL This exercise is the basis from which you can develop your heading skills. Stand facing a wall, about one metre away from it. Using both hands, hold the ball up to the **centre** of your forehead, well clear of your nose. With your **eyes open**, bring your head back and arch your back. Now strike the ball out of your hands, against the wall, with your forehead. Practise this until you can recognise which part of your forehead you need to use and how bringing your head back gives power and direction to the ball.

Now imagine that the ball is coming to you from your right. Turn your body slightly to the right and place your left foot forwards, as in fig. 28. You can still head the ball forward with your body facing another way because you are directing the ball **with your forehead**, which should be facing **towards the wall**. Next, imagine the ball is coming from the left by placing your right foot forwards and heading the ball.

Practise Other Headers
You can use this method to practise other headers, for example a high ball. Hold the ball higher and look up, as in fig. 29a. Bring the ball towards your forehead and, at the same time, arch your back. Now attack the ball with your forehead (fig. 29b).

Fig. 28 Turn to the right with your left foot forwards. Keep the ball at the centre of your forehead.

Fig. 29 a) Hold the ball high and look up . . .
b) . . .the ball is returned high in the air by the direction and power of your forehead.

Build up your Confidence in Heading the Ball

PUPIL   When the ball is travelling fast, the timing of your forehead contact is very important, but you will need time to practise this. **Always keep your eyes open and meet the ball with your forehead**. You may blink naturally on contact with the ball, but you should always be able to see where the ball is coming from and, afterwards, where it is going (don't miss seeing your goal go in!).

TEACHER   Stand facing the pupil, 3–4 metres away from him. Gently throw the ball underarm and slightly higher than his head. The pupil should then head the ball back to you, using the same technique as with the wall practice. Tell him to head the ball back to you, first at eye level (fig. 30), and then progressively higher in the air.

Fig. 30   Heading the ball back at eye level.

Vary the Headers
Now tell the pupil to head the ball towards the right or the left. Let him head the ball towards a wall – this will give him a target to aim at, and will save time in collecting the ball.

    Now tell the pupil whether to head the ball high (fig. 31) or low, and throw the ball from either side of the pupil (fig. 32).

Fig. 31 Heading the ball higher.

Increase the Distance
Still throwing underarm, slightly increase the distance between you and the pupil. If you are in any doubt about the pupil's performance, go back to some simpler headers and work up to the harder exercises again.

Fig. 32 Heading the ball down.

LESSON 5

THE SIDE-FOOT PASS

We now move on to passing the ball, using the inside of your foot. You can practise this after the stretching exercises, and whilst warming up. The following method is fairly straightforward, although very different to striking the ball. Do not try anything fancy at this stage.

TEACHER Demonstrate the following kick to the pupil, making sure to emphasise the difference between side-foot passing and striking the ball. The pupil must use alternate feet.

PUPIL Walk up to the ball (from almost directly behind it) and turn your **right foot outwards to make a right angle with your left foot**, as shown in fig. 33. **Use the area of the side of your foot midway between the toe and the heel to kick the ball with a fast lower leg movement** (fig. 34). Moving your foot fast means that you hit the ball harder. **Hit the middle of the ball so that it will travel straight and low**. Practise against a wall to see what level of accuracy and firmness you can achieve. Use your right, then your left foot and so on.

Using your Left and Right Foot

PUPIL Have you seen some of the great players take penalties? Well, try this. With your teacher as goalkeeper, place the ball on the penalty spot and walk back 2–3 metres,

Fig. 33   Turn your foot to make a right angle with the other foot.

Fig. 34   Keeping your eye on the ball, pass the ball with a fast, hard tap.

directly behind the ball (fig. 35). **Stop**. Look at where you will aim your shot (low, and about 50–100 cm inside the post). Now jog up to the ball. **Place one foot alongside the ball, keep your eye on the ball,** then side-foot the ball in the same manner as you have been practising. Practise using your left and right foot, but also **aim either side of the goalkeeper.** (These variations are not easy.)

Fig. 35 Practise using your right and left foot.

AN INTRODUCTION TO THE SECOND SET OF LESSONS

PUPIL

- Have your practised all the skills in lessons 1 to 5?
- How confident are you?
- Can you execute the skills correctly?
- Have you improved?

If in any doubt, practise more before you continue . . .

If you were to compare a local league football match with a National League game, you'd see that there is a great variation in the levels of skill exhibited. However, the physical aspects of play may differ little at times. Some of the players in the lower league teams may be able to match the straightforward running speed of the National League players.

Whether or not he can run fast, a football player's priority must be the development of his skills. The longer you leave it, the harder these are to acquire. The more you rely on your speed as a youngster, the less likely you are to control your speed when you are older. The best way to play is with quick, agile ball control, or short bursts of speed, but first you will need to focus more on your technique.

TEACHER   Youngsters need help in nurturing their abilities. This involves patience and the teaching of discipline. All children have a tendency to get excited when they run around with the ball, often quickly losing interest and becoming bored. At times, you will need to remain calm and add some fun into the practice. Children are able to learn things a lot quicker than adults, so make sure you explain the procedures correctly in order to keep them in good stead for when they are older.

The next lessons will highlight the need to practise hard. Do not spend too much time on any one lesson. Go through each exercise three or four times before moving on, but be prepared to go back and repeat the whole sequence. If he is keen, the pupil will want to go back and perfect all the lessons anyway. The lessons are in a set sequence, so do not skip ahead. As you warm up, recap on some of the previous lessons.

PUPIL   If you are currently playing for a team, read the final part of the book before you play your next game. This will help you to understand how to play steadily in a game and also what you are supposed to be doing on the pitch.

We now move on to the next set of lessons. Some of these will need a reasonably competent person who can kick the ball and perform tricks, like handstands and cartwheels. No, only joking – I'm sure dad will be fine!

LESSON 6

STRIKING THE BALL WITH GREATER PRECISION

PUPIL Stand facing a wall, about 5–7 metres away from it. (Now tap your foot on the ground impatiently while your teacher is reading the next section.) You will strike the ball from the same position throughout this lesson. You may notice that the phrase "gentle strike" has disappeared; however, if you miss the target, go back to striking gently. Remember: power comes later! **Use the centre (lace area) of your boot to strike the middle part of the ball (or just above).** This will help keep the ball low. The position of your foot also guides the ball low, so **point your toes down**. As ever, keep your eye on the ball.

TEACHER Stand nearer than the pupil to the wall, but to one side of him. Facing the pupil, pass a steady ball along the ground towards him, as shown in fig. 36. The pupil should then strike the moving ball and shoot at the target area on the wall. Pass the ball from the pupil's **right side** so that he uses his **right foot to strike the ball**. Now pass the ball from the pupil's **left side** so that he uses his **left foot to strike the ball** (fig. 37). Do not vary the procedure with this lesson.

Receiving a Pass From the Side

TEACHER Both you and the pupil should stand 5–7 metres away from a wall, but about 3–4 metres apart from

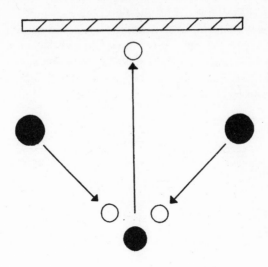

Fig. 36 Teacher passes the ball.
Pupil shoots at target.

Fig. 37 The teacher passes from the left side ... and the pupil shoots
with his left foot. Strike the middle to top part of the ball to keep
it low.

each other. Pass the ball to the pupil, as in fig. 38. The pupil now receives the ball from the side and should strike it against the wall. Pass the ball from either side of the pupil. When being passed a ball from his right side, the pupil should use his right foot to strike; when passed from the left, he should use his left foot to hit the ball, as in fig. 39.

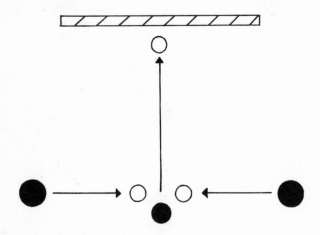

Fig. 38 Teacher passes ball from either side.
Pupil shoots the ball forwards.

Fig. 39 A pass from the left side – the pupil uses his left foot to strike the ball.

Receiving a Pass From the Rear

TEACHER Now stand slightly behind the pupil, but still to one side (fig. 40). Pass the ball from the pupil's right (as in fig. 41) and left side as before. The pupil needs to strike the ball low and precisely into the goal. Remind him, "eye on the ball – strike!"

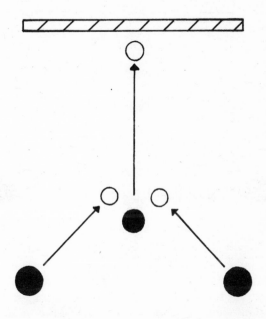

Fig. 40 Teacher passes the ball from slightly behind the pupil.

This exercise makes it more difficult for the pupil to strike a moving ball. It is good practice for his balance and timing, and it tests his ability to strike the ball using either foot.

The Half Volley
For this, the pass needs to be accurate and the strike somewhat faster. This type of exercise will show the importance of correct timing and precision, as well as the need for quick

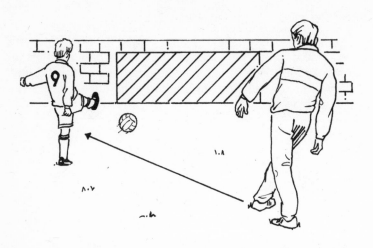

Fig. 41 Teacher passes the ball from the right side. The pupil strikes the
ball low, using his right foot.

reflex actions. For the moment, only spend a short time on this
exercise.

TEACHER   Take up the same positions as in the previous
exercise, but move closer to the pupil. Throw the ball under
arm (below waist height) towards the pupil's foot, **allowing
the ball to hit the ground just before reaching his foot**. The
pupil should then use a **short but swift strike** to hit the ball
against the wall.

Throw the ball from all six positions, as in fig. 42. Tell the
pupil to **arch his body** over the ball, keeping his **toes down**
and his **eye on the ball**.

PUPIL   Immediately the ball bounces up, strike it towards
the wall. You must use your left or right foot, depending on
what side the ball comes to you from. Look for the bounce
then execute a **short swift strike**, as in fig. 43. This will give
you a feel for the quick lower leg movement which provides
accuracy with some power.

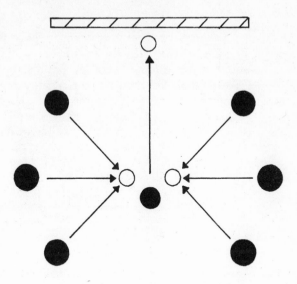

Fig. 42 Teacher throws the ball from all six positions.

Fig. 43 Teacher throws the ball to hit the ground just before it reaches the pupil's foot.

Full Volleys in the Six Positions

TEACHER Take up the same position as in the previous exercise, but **move a lot closer to the pupil**. Throw the ball underarm so that it lands directly onto the pupil's foot. He should then strike the ball low into the goal. Throw the ball gently and accurately from all six positions, three either side of the pupil, as shown in fig. 44. The pupil must execute all of these strikes correctly (at least once) before he moves on.

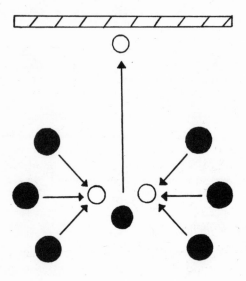

Fig. 44 Teacher moves closer and throws the ball from all six positions.

PUPIL Your shot needs to be low. Anybody can whack a ball in the air! **You need to use the lace area of your boot, but aim low so the ball travels either level or towards the ground**, as in fig. 45.

Fig. 45 Teacher throws the ball so it lands on the pupil's foot.
Pupil strikes the ball low into the goal.

TEACHER From the last three exercises you can now judge the pupil's ability to strike the ball. These are good tests of skill, some difficult to execute. If the pupil has taken the shots correctly, this is good news; if not, **practice makes perfect**.

Look at the Sequence

TEACHER Football skills need to be taught in a set sequence, as a similar pattern of events will also take place in a top class game. Unless you point the sequence out, it is easily left unnoticed or forgotten. The most common sequence is when a player receives the ball ⇨ quickly controls it ⇨ lifts his head ⇨ decides on his action ⇨ then executes his play. Any sequence of events is important to learn as it will steady the pupil and help him to assess the play around him. So the older and quicker he gets, the more controlled his reactions will be.

LESSON 7

TERRIFIC REFLEX ACTIONS

TEACHER Can you pass a ball over a short distance accurately? Face the pupil, 5–7 metres away from him and pass a **fast** ball along the ground to him. The pupil will need to watch the speed of the ball, then **bring his foot back to cushion the ball**. He must use **alternate feet** to trap the ball.

PUPIL Keeping your eye on the ball, **lean forwards and relax**. Bring your foot back at the moment of impact to cushion the speed of the ball and limit the bounce.

Speed Up the Control

TEACHER Face the pupil, about 8–10 metres away from him. Tell him to turn to face the other way (fig. 46a). Now pass a fast ball towards the pupil, at the same time calling "**turn**". Limit the amount of time the pupil has to turn and trap the ball. Tell the pupil "**head up**" as he controls the ball. If he has difficulties, tell him to turn quicker, otherwise call "turn" sooner well before the ball reaches him – this will give him more time to react.

PUPIL
1. Quickly turn and control the ball, as in fig. 46b.
2. **Get your head up, look left then right.**
3. **Wait a few seconds**.
4. Now look back down to the ball.
5. Use the **inside** of your foot to pass back to the teacher, as in fig. 46c.

Fig. 46 a) Pupil has his back to the teacher and waits for the command "turn".
b) Pupil quickly turns to control the ball.
c) Pupil quickly lifts his head then looks left and right before passing the ball back to the teacher.

Make sure to follow this five part sequence in order.

Fig. 47 Turning anticlockwise and clockwise.

Turn the Pupil Either Way

| TEACHER | Still with the same exercise, this time, before you call "turn", tell the pupil whether he is to turn anticlockwise or clockwise (fig. 47).

- Now tell the pupil which foot to trap the ball with before you give the command "turn".
- For teachers who find it difficult to pass the ball fast along the ground, throw or drop-kick the ball to the pupil. This could be a high (fig. 48) or low ball, but tell the pupil with which foot to control the ball and which way to turn before you deliver the ball.

Fig. 48 A higher ball, but still aimed towards the pupil's feet.

- **The most important factor is how the pupil reacts and gains control of the ball. He must move quickly, but relax when the ball nears him.**

These movements will help ball control and composure.

| PUPIL | A ball in the air is harder to control than one along the ground, so this exercise will keep you on your toes. After turning, keep your eye on the ball ⇨ move quickly ⇨ then relax.

LESSON 8

ONE-TO-ONE PLAY

The next lesson requires coolness as well as agility and shows the need for players to think and steady their actions. **The younger the pupil the more strictly the rules must be adhered to**.

For this lesson you only need a small playing area, about 6m long by 5m wide or even smaller. Make up goals 75cm wide (or use kit bags) at either end of the 'pitch'. The first part of this lesson is devoted to attacking. Ten minute practices are adequate.

TEACHER **Do not tackle the pupil**. The pupil must feel confident against an opponent, so allow him 90% possession of the ball. Let him experiment with side moves, turning you one way then the other. Allow the pupil to go past you, but from his own initiative. Do not let the pupil shoot from a distance. Keep within this small area and, if you are unfit or as old as I am, take it easy and let him do most of the work! Remind the pupil, "**head up**".

PUPIL This is a good opportunity for you to gain confidence on the ball. **Try at all times to move the ball into a space away from the teacher**. Sometimes roll the ball backwards, but mainly move sideways, left then right and so on, until a space has opened up for you to go forward. **Keep the ball away from the teacher using quick side to side movements**, moving one or two metres only. Make the most of this exercise; practise the following skills:

Fig. 49 Off-balance the teacher and pretend to strike the ball.

- Pretend that you are going to strike the ball, but stop your foot just before it reaches it. This pretence may allow you to off-balance the teacher (fig. 49), then push the ball behind him. Pretend to strike the ball with your left and then your right foot.
- With the ball at your feet, pretend you are going to run to the right or the left by taking a step in that direction. Put your shoulder down to make it look more convincing. Then take the ball the other way, as in fig. 50. Practise this either way and you will confuse the teacher.
- Place the ball in front of you and step one foot sideways over it. Now use the same foot to tap the ball sideways. The direction in which you step over the ball will determine whether you use the inside or outside of your foot to tap the ball. Practise this with your right and left feet. Use this trick combined with body movements and you will definitely confuse the teacher! (See fig. 51.)

Fig. 50 Confuse the teacher then take the ball the other way.

Fig. 51 Pupil steps over the ball and teacher leans the same way. Pupil takes the ball in the other direction. Keep your head up.

You must keep your head up and look to see if you are confusing the teacher. If not, make the pretence look more convincing. Practise with alternate feet and let your body sway to emphasise the deception.

One-to-One Defending

TEACHER We now have a slight variation from the previous exercise. Teacher, how good are you on the ball? You are now the attacker. Try to confuse the pupil with some tricks. You will need possession of the ball at least 50% of the time. Encourage the pupil **not to dive in and tackle you** – tell him to jockey you and **be patient**. The pupil must stay on his feet, keep on his toes, watch the ball and wait for the right moment to tackle you. In the future, he is sure to come up against some skilful opponents, so this is good practice.

PUPIL Practise defending in a one-to-one situation correctly. **Do not rush any tackles unless you are certain of winning the ball**. Mistakes look clumsy and can lose your team a game. The best way to keep a good attacker at bay or to win the ball is to **anticipate his movements**. Try to be patient, watching to see if the teacher makes an error. Turn at the same speed as he, keeping about one metre away from him. Keep your eye on the ball

More One-to-One Practice

TEACHER You must practise one-to-one play regularly, but only in a 2–3 metre area. This will help to steady the pupil's ball control in tight situations.

Face the pupil, 1 metre away from him. Tell him to **move sideways with the ball**, left then right and so on (fig. 52). Follow the pupil's movements, but **do not tackle him**. You may, however, clip the ball from his feet every now and then. The pupil's movements must stay **within 2–3 metres**. Tell him to keep his head up, especially if he is young. As the pupil's ability increases, force him to work harder to keep the ball, but take it easy – don't wear yourself out!

Fig. 52   Keep your head up and move sideways with the ball.

PUPIL   Vary your movements to the left and to the right to try to off-balance the teacher. Look for an opportunity to push the ball past the teacher or through his legs (fig. 53). Stop every now and then and pretend that you are going to move to one side. Your teacher will follow you and he may open his legs just enough for you to push the ball between them. Keep your head up before and after any move.

TEACHER   Face the pupil and let him have possession of the ball. Move slowly towards the pupil in a brief attempt to take the ball. The pupil should roll the ball backwards away from you, using the sole of his boot. Then, at an opportune moment, he should take the ball either to the left or the right. The pupil must use **alternate feet to roll the ball backwards** (fig. 54), but he can use either foot to tap the ball sideways.

PUPIL   With this exercise, roll the ball back only one metre, then take the ball sideways. Try to **speed up this action without losing control of the ball**.

Fig. 53 Look for an opportunity to push the ball through the teacher's legs. Keep your head up before and after any move.

Fig. 54 Use alternate feet to roll the ball backwards.

LESSON 9

MORE CIRCLE MOVEMENTS

PUPIL Do you remember the imaginary circle in lesson 3? Well, you are going to jog around it again. Your teacher will stand in the middle of the circle and throw or kick the ball to you. Keep your **head up** at all times, apart from when you are controlling or striking the ball.

TEACHER Tell the pupil to jog **clockwise** around the imaginary circle. Call "**control**" and, at the same time, throw the ball (over arm) just in front of the pupil's feet (fig. 55). The pupil should control the ball ⇨ jog a few paces ⇨ then smoothly strike the ball back to you using his left foot.

Fig. 55 Teacher calls "control" and throws the ball in front of the pupil's feet. Pupil jogs clockwise, so he uses his left foot to receive the ball and pass it back.

Now tell the pupil to jog **anticlockwise**, so he uses his **right foot** to strike the ball back to you. You can give the command "**turn**" at any time. If you are able to kick an accurate ball, pass it along the ground to the pupil. Use this method at random moments.

- Still with the same exercise, tell the pupil to pass the ball back to you using the **inside** of his foot.
- Again with the same exercise, tell the pupil to control the ball ⇨ take it in small circles, clockwise or anticlockwise (as in lesson 3) ⇨ then pass or strike the ball back to you.

Tell the pupil what to do before he starts jogging and make one change after each full circle.

Meeting the Ball

| TEACHER | Often, in soccer matches, children wait for the ball to arrive at their feet when it is passed to them, or they run forwards when expecting to receive a pass from behind. Whilst both actions occur frequently in top level soccer, they may prove to be a hindrance to a young player. Lack of forethought or unnecessary forward runs will not help a young player progress. With this in mind, practise meeting the ball regularly, so that the pupil learns how to meet a ball correctly from any direction.

LESSON 10

THROW INS AND MEETING THE BALL

We now see some throw ins and meeting the ball. This lesson will combine ball control with game tactics, so increasing the pupil's need to really think about what is going on around him.

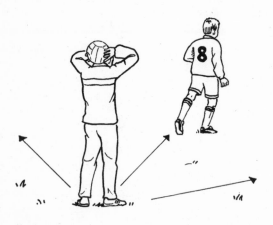

Fig. 56 Pupil jogs away from teacher and waits for the command "turn".

<u>TEACHER</u> Hold the ball behind your head as if to take a throw in towards the pupil. Now tell the pupil to turn and jog

away from you (fig. 56), with his back to you. When you are ready, call "**turn**". The pupil should turn to face you then jog towards you. Now choose a sensible moment to throw the ball towards the pupil's feet. He should meet the moving ball and make a first time pass back to you. Vary the direction in which the pupil jogs: straight in front of you, to your left and to your right. Throw the ball low towards the ground and limit the amount of bounce.

Now repeat the exercise, but this time ask the pupil to **sprint** towards you.

Note: you may find it difficult to throw the ball at the correct time for the pupil, or the ball may bounce awkwardly. If so, use the same exercise as above but pass the ball along the ground instead of throwing in. This will serve as a good way of promoting a meeting with the ball.

Fig. 57 Pupil abruptly slows down and passes a first time ball back to teacher.

PUPIL   Keep your eye on the ball. Pass a first time ball back to the teacher using the most convenient foot. Always

slow down when you meet the ball so that you can pass accurately (fig. 57). When you have completed all of these variations you must **swap positions** with the teacher and practise a few throw ins yourself. Throw the ball in towards the teacher sensibly – you don't need to knock him out!

More Throw Ins

| TEACHER | Use the same three directions and tell the pupil to turn and sprint towards you as before. Again, this will show the need for the pupil to steady his pace when meeting the ball.

a   b   c

Fig. 58 a) Trap the ball then pass back to teacher.
            b) Trap the ball then turn and dribble the ball away from teacher.
            c) Tap the ball to one side using your left and right feet.

Using these same throw ins:
- Tell the pupil to **trap the ball**, then swiftly **make the pass** to you, as in fig. 58a.
- Tell the pupil to **trap the ball**, then turn and **dribble it away** from you, as in fig. 58b.

● Tell the pupil to **tap the moving ball gently to one side** using the inside of his foot, as in fig. 58c. He should practise using either foot, so he taps the ball left or right, then tell him to run a few metres with it.

Note: Again, these throws will be difficult to perfect so try passing the ball along the ground as well.

Throw Ins to the Chest and Forehead

 TEACHER We'll now try a throw for the more advanced pupil. This must be taken with the pupil fairly close to you. Throw the ball gently onto the pupil's chest, and he should use his chest firmly to direct the ball back to your feet, as in fig. 59a. (For the younger pupils, 'chesting' the ball is in the next lesson.)

Fig. 59 a) Firmly chest the ball back to teacher.
b) A positive header back to teacher.

Now take some throw ins directly onto the pupil's forehead. Tell him to head the ball back to your feet (fig. 59b). Are you getting fed up with throwing the ball yet?

The Longer Throw In

It is now the pupil's turn to practise *throwing* some throw ins. It is important for the pupil to master a longer throw as one day he may find himself in a situation where this type of throw is needed.

PUPIL   You may now practise some longer throw ins, but do not use this type of throw if you want the ball to be passed back to you!

Hold the ball correctly to get a feel for the action.

- Spread your fingers to the side of and behind the ball, your thumbs at the bottom pointing towards each other.
- Bring the ball up behind your head and, at the same time, bend your knees as in fig. 60a.
- You should feel the tension in your wrists as your fingers are level behind you. If not, twist your wrists back towards the ground.

a   b   c

Fig. 60   a) Twist wrists to get a feel for the direction. Bend knees and bring elbows slightly forward.

b) Thrust the ball up and forward.

c) Walking forward with the ball, bring feet together and then thrust the ball.

- Holding this position, bend your knees and keep your elbows slightly forward. You should now feel you can throw the ball up in the air.

The thrust.

- Practise slowly to start with so that you get a good feel for this action, but the faster you can propel the ball from your hands the further it will travel.

- Starting from a static position, twist your wrist and rock the ball back and forth, as if to throw the ball. This will give you a sense of direction.

- Now bend your knees and thrust the ball up and forward using a fast action from your arms. The upwards and forwards movement should leave you with your hands in the air, like the boy in fig. 60b.

- Now try doing the same action while walking forwards. As you are about to throw the ball, bring your feet together and thrust the ball, as in fig. 60c.

LESSON 11

OTHER THROW IN EXERCISES

This lesson is useful for enhancing ball control and it allows a bit of fun in the process!

Trapping a High or Low Ball onto your Chest

| TEACHER | Stand facing the pupil, a few metres away from him. Throw the ball onto the ground so it bounces towards the pupil in the air. You can judge the speed of the ball from the bounce and make the ball go either low or high in the air. Take care how you direct the ball if your pupil is young.

| PUPIL | When the ball is upon you, lean back and cushion the ball with your chest, as in fig. 61a.

To trap a low ball with your chest, lean forward when the ball is upon you, arch your shoulders and then direct the ball to the ground, as in fig. 61b.

More Ways to Control the Ball

| TEACHER | Face the pupil and either bounce the ball onto the ground or throw the ball in the air. As the ball comes down, the pupil should cushion the ball using the lace area of his boot. This will only be effective if he raises his foot under the ball and then brings it down at the same speed as the ball, as in fig. 62a. Practise using alternate feet.

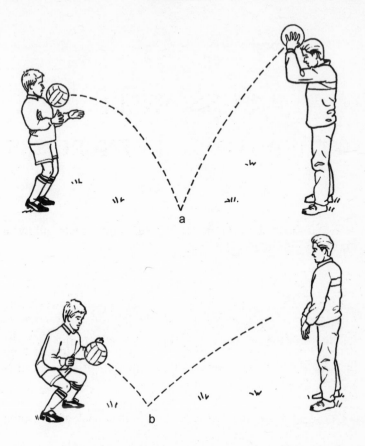

Fig. 61 a) Pupil leans **back** to cushion a high ball.
b) Pupil leans **forward** to cushion a low ball.

Now bounce the ball so the pupil cushions the ball using his thighs, as in fig. 62b. As soon as the ball hits the pupil's thigh, tell him to straighten his leg. The ball will then drop to the ground near to the pupil's feet (fig. 62c).

Heading a Fast-Moving Ball

 TEACHER Throw the ball overarm for the pupil to head (fig. 63a). Start by throwing the ball gently, then increase the

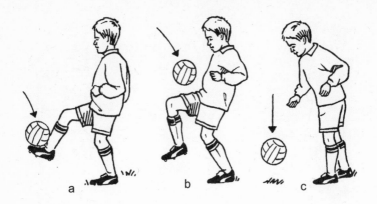

Fig. 62   a) Pupil lowers his foot to cushion the ball.
           b) Pupil raises his thigh to meet the ball.
           c) Pupil straightens his leg and the ball drops to the ground.

speed of the ball up to a reasonably testing pace. See how well the pupil copes, but be careful not to discourage him by pushing him too far. Move closer to the pupil so his reactions become quicker. This practice could take place with the pupil heading the ball onto a wall or high into the air. Refer back to the instructions for headers in lesson 4, page 38-42. Do not try this exercise if the pupil is young. Older pupils need only practise this minimally.

PUPIL   You need to keep your eye on the ball and meet the ball with your forehead (fig. 63b). Your forehead should always end up facing the direction in which you want the ball to go.

Fig. 63 a) Throwing a fast ball.
b) The centre of the forehead directs the ball.

LESSON 12

SPECIAL WAYS OF STRIKING THE BALL

One quality of a great player is the ability to strike the ball using either foot, making the ball go where they want it to go, how they want it to go: high, low, long, swerving, fast or steady. Sounds difficult? Well, even some top players struggle to use either foot and do not always play the ball that accurately. Therefore, to be able to strike the ball low using either foot is a good start for any youngster.

Some Facts on Lifting the Ball
We are often told that, in order to lift the ball off the ground, we must lean back. Well, this is not necessary and may confuse your actions. Leaning back will occur naturally, just after you strike the ball. To prove the point, stand upright and bring your kicking leg all the way back and then forwards in one big sweep, as if to strike the ball. In this movement your body will follow a natural course: you will first lean forwards (fig. 64a) and then backwards (fig. 64b).

We can either limit or emphasise our body movements in order to control a shot. For example, we lean over the ball to keep a shot low and we stand upright then force ourselves back to lift the ball high. However, this does not always mean that the ball will travel where we want it to go. Therefore, how our foot makes contact with the ball is the deciding factor for the ball's direction of travel.

Fig. 64 Bring the kicking leg back and forth – see how your body leans.
a) Leg back – you lean forward.
b) Leg forwards – you lean back.

PUPIL Try exaggerating the way the ball is lifted. Bring your leg back and bend your knee so that your foot is behind you and almost parallel to the ground, as in fig. 65a. Now use a sweeping action to strike the ball, turning your heel inwards and directing your foot well under the ball so your foot comes closer to the ground and hits the lower part of the ball (fig. 65b).

Practise this from a static starting position, and then by walking up to the ball first. See if you can make the ball travel straight and rise high off the ground. If you keep your eye on the ball and make the correct contact you should chip the ball well off the ground. Still use the lace area of your boot and practise using alternate feet.

TEACHER Stand alongside the pupil. Make sure that the action is correct, then get him to chip the ball to you.

Striking with Power

TEACHER We will now shift the emphasis to encouraging a strike with power. Note that trying to hit the ball in this

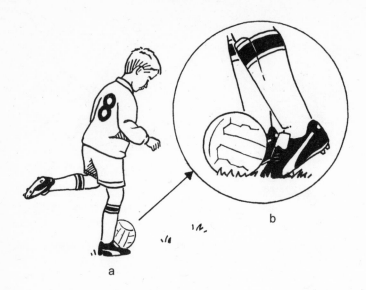

Fig. 65 a) Bring foot back almost parallel to the ground – heel inwards.
b) Direct your foot well under the ball.

manner is not a good idea for youngsters as, for them, accuracy is more important.

PUPIL   This is different from the last exercise as you do not need to achieve lift. You may use power in conjunction with any method of striking the ball. But remember – how your foot makes contact with the ball will determine in which direction the ball travels.

- To strike the ball low with power, keep your eye on the middle part of the ball but focus more on your foot gaining speed as it makes contact with the ball (fig. 66a). Really smack the ball hard. Your foot should follow through, waist high, with your leg ending up straight, as in fig. 66b. We sometimes see a player striking the ball so hard that both feet come off the ground as the force of the follow through has momentarily lifted his body off the ground!

a   b

Fig. 66 a) Focus more on your foot gaining speed.
b) Follow through fast. Your leg should end up straight.

Fig. 67 Rapidly increase the speed of your foot. Make sure the ball travels straight and fast.

- You will only get power behind the ball when you force an impact. You will not be able to force any impact on the ball unless the speed of your foot rapidly increases. To explain this further: bring your leg back, then slowly forward, but rapidly increase the speed of your foot as it lowers towards the ball. This acceleration will create a strong impact. Practise this method from a static starting position to get a feel for the action. You can emphasise your body action by leaning forward to keep the ball low. Strike your foot to the middle part of the ball and make sure the ball travels quite fast and straight (fig. 67).

Fig. 68 If your body is relaxed you will naturally lean back. The ball leaves your foot fast from a good foot contact.

- Now smartly step a few paces up to the ball and use a more continuous leg action, but really smack the ball hard, following through with your leg swiftly. This action will cause you to lean back, as in fig. 68, so make sure you have a good foot contact to produce the correct effect. You must keep your **eye on the ball**.

The Long Ball with Lift

PUPIL The way to gain lift and distance from the ball is to strike your foot just below the middle of the ball and use some power.

We have practised chipping the ball to achieve a high lift previously (page 78/9). If your foot strikes just below the middle of the ball this will lift the ball, but less. Yet if you add power, the ball will rise steadily and the lift will increase.

Fig. 69 Fix your eyes just below the middle of the ball. This will make it easier to hit the ball correctly.

Jog up to the ball from only a few paces away and fix your eyes just below the middle of the ball (fig. 69). Where you place your non-striking foot will make a big difference. If it is too far forward this may reduce your power and thus the lifting effect. If your foot is placed too far behind the ball you will need to stretch to reach it, in which case again you may reduce your power, or even fall over. For the best strike, place your non-striking foot alongside the ball and powerfully strike the ball off the ground (fig. 70).

TEACHER Whacking the ball to gain power and lift is **not** a good idea to practise too much, especially if the child is

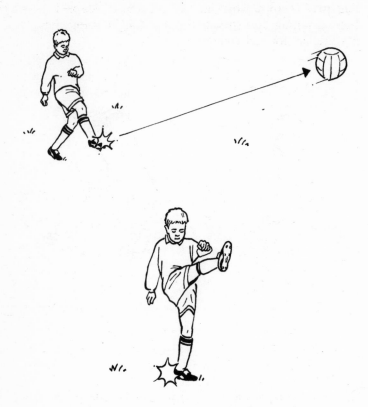

Fig. 70   Use some power – the ball will travel and rise steadily off the ground.

young. For him to know what to do with the ball and produce some effect is adequate.

Curling the Ball

 TEACHER Using the lace area of the boot provides many options. The player can curl the ball either left or right and may use this action with lift or power. However, if a child is young, it is better not to attempt these variations too soon as this may disrupt what he has previously learned or may become boring. Just striking the ball straight, using either foot, is sufficient for real youngsters.

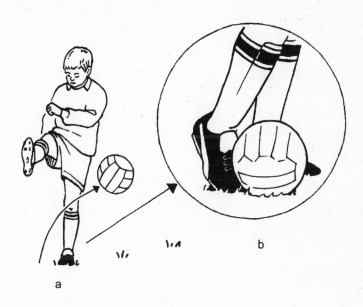

Fig. 71 a) Follow your foot through and round in front of you.
b) Strike the ball using the inner part of your boot.

PUPIL   To make the ball curl inward, strike the ball using the **inner** part of your boot, near the lace holes (fig. 71b). Practise by first standing alongside the ball so you get a feel for the action. Aim your foot **just below the middle part of the ball** and follow your foot through (fig. 71a). Practise using alternate feet.

Now jog up to the ball and, approaching the ball more from the side, use some power (fig. 72).

To curl the ball outward, strike the ball using the **outer** part of your foot near the lace holes (fig. 73c). As before, follow

Fig. 72 Approach the ball more from the side. Jog up to the ball and use some power.

your foot through as you strike (fig. 73b). This type of strike will not produce any effect unless the ball travels low, with power, and ends up spot on target. This strike can look like a mis-kick if it's not really accurate, but it is worth practising with either foot. Try the approach in fig. 73a opposite.

Using the Top and Outer Part of your Foot

PUPIL Stand with your feet 15 cm apart. Turn your right foot inwards and kick the ball forward using the top and outer part of your foot, as in fig. 74a. You will perhaps feel awkward performing this type of kick, but practise using either foot. You will eventually get a feel for the movement and will be able to hit the ball with some power, following your foot through (fig. 74b). This type of kick is useful to pass or direct the ball quickly in certain situations.

TEACHER This method of kicking the ball is a different technique again to what has already been learned, so be sure to

Fig. 73 a) A typical approach using the right foot.
b) Follow your foot through.
c) Use the outer part of your boot.

Fig. 74 a) Use either foot and build up to hitting the ball with power.
b) Use the top and outer part of your boot.

keep it separate from other exercises.

Juggling with the Ball

 PUPIL   This is an exercise you may know already. Juggling with the ball will help your balance and ball control, yet it is only seen as pre-match flair. This is quite difficult to do with both feet, let alone with your head, thighs, shoulders, arms and back. Juggling may take some time to master, but it is worth practising. However, you don't juggle with the ball during a game so, if you do not become an expert, so what?

Use the sole of your boot to pull the ball backwards (fig. 75a), then flick it up in the air using the lace area of your boot. Try to keep the ball a short distance from the ground and flick the ball towards you. Now use alternate feet to keep it up in the air (fig. 75b). You could try:

Fig. 75 a) Roll the ball backwards.
b) Flick the ball up a short distance from the ground. Use alternate feet.

●   keeping the ball up in the air using the top of your thighs or forehead (fig. 76)
●   juggling the ball from one part of your body to another
●   or walking forwards while keeping the ball up in the air.
These are not very easy, so only try juggling for short periods of time. Then, if you are really good, get ready for the circus!

While on the subject of being a flash player, try this useful back pass. Walk away from the teacher with the ball and then use your heel to jab the ball back. Use alternate feet.

Side Foot Practice

| **TEACHER** | Remember lesson 1, where you threw the ball to the pupil and he would gently strike it back to you? This exercise is similar, except the pupil uses the side of his foot to pass the ball back into your arms.

Fig. 76 You could keep the ball in the air using your forehead

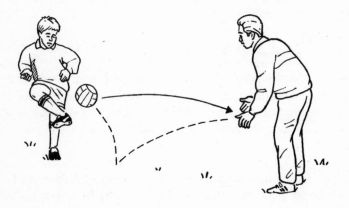

Fig. 77 Pupil uses the side of his foot to pass the ball into teacher's arms.

Start by bouncing the ball in front of him and then move on to throwing the ball directly onto his foot. The pupil should use alternate feet to side foot the ball back to you, as in fig. 77.

LESSON 13

MOVE AND SHOOT

This next lesson will bring your skills into play, but will also show you the need for poise. A change of pace from quick to slow is extremely important in soccer. With these exercises, try to use a soccer pitch and a goal.

TEACHER The pupil will strike the ball from four different positions: left of the goal, either side of centre, and right of the goal. Your job is to be the goalkeeper, or to stand behind the goal to collect any missed balls. Tell the pupil to dribble fast, but make sure he **changes his pace** and **steadies up** before striking the ball. Composure and accuracy are vital, not power.

PUPIL Stand outside the penalty area and dribble the ball fast towards the goal (fig. 78a). **Keep your head up**. As you approach the goal, **abruptly slow down** and take your time with the shot. Tap the ball forward but very slightly to one side as you are about to shoot (fig. 78b). It is more effective to position the ball correctly first than to move sideways to strike the ball. Hit the **middle part** of the ball to keep it low. Use your right foot to strike the ball, as in fig. 78c.

- Follow the same sequence from the four different positions shown in fig. 79.
- Now execute the four shots from the four positions, but this time use your **left foot**. You weren't trying to get away without doing that, were you?

Fig. 78 a) Dribble ball fast towards the goal . . .
b) . . . abruptly slow down and tap ball slightly diagonally . . .
c) . . . strike the middle of the ball.

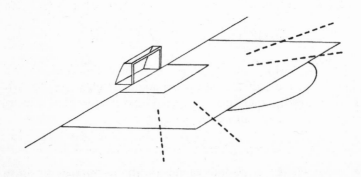

Fig. 79 Strike from four different positions.

Speed up the Control and Take Time with the Shot

The importance of a change is now demonstrated again in a new exercise, still in the goal area. This further highlights the need for composure and for the pupil to tap the ball forward before striking. This exercise is **not** a model for how to score at close range, but features controlled striking.

Fig. 80   Teacher kicks a high ball.

TEACHER   Stand in goal and ask the pupil to stand beyond the penalty spot. Throw or kick a high ball to the pupil, as in fig. 80. The pupil **must** follow the sequence below and do it with alternate feet: first the left foot to control and strike the ball, next time the right foot to control and strike the ball. After all, we don't want things too easy for him! While the pupil is having fun he also needs a good test.

PUPIL   Move quickly and control the ball ⇨ look up (fig. 81) ⇨ tap the ball forward and perhaps slightly to one side (only a touch, otherwise you may lose valuable time chasing after it, fig. 82) ⇨ strike the ball (fig. 83).

Speed Up the Control but Maintain the Composure

TEACHER   To reinforce further the techniques learnt in the previous exercise, tell the pupil to turn and face the other way (fig. 84) then throw or kick the ball. Give the command

Fig. 81 Pupil moves quickly ⇨ controls ball ⇨ lifts head up.

Fig. 82 Pupil taps the ball slightly forward.

Fig. 83 Pupil strikes ball at goal.

''**turn**''. The pupil needs to quickly turn ⇨ control the ball ⇨ lift up his head ⇨ tap the ball forward ⇨ then execute the strike. **Make sure the pupil follows this sequence.**

Fig. 84 The pupil turns his back to the teacher and follows the sequence.

- Now vary the height and speed of the ball. Make the pupil work to control the ball.
- Now tell the pupil to stand well to the side of the goal and do the same (fig. 85). This position will narrow his shooting angle and remind the pupil of the importance of **lifting his head**. In a game, another member of his team might be in a good scoring position, so a side pass may be better!

Fig. 85 The pupil stands well to the side of the goal and receives the ball, lifting his head to see whether a cross or a pass is an option.

LESSON 14

THE RETURN BALL

This next lesson is again in the goal area (or against a wall with a small target area), but with passing moves this time. This will give another insight into making first time passes and the importance of playing the ball the way you are facing. These moves may seem quite basic, but do not underestimate their value. This type of play can arise in many situations all over the pitch.

Fig. 86 Teacher passes and pupil meets the ball.

TEACHER Look at fig. 86. Stand beyond the penalty spot and face the goal. Position the pupil, facing you, near the goal post to your left. Throw or kick a low, bouncing ball towards the pupil, then move a few paces forward. The pupil should run to meet the ball, then pass it back, using his right foot, so you can shoot with your left foot. Only shoot if you want to. Now make it easier and pass the ball to the pupil along the ground. Alternate between a bouncing ball and a pass along the ground.

Fig. 87 Pupil passes the ball using right foot. Teacher uses left foot to shoot at target.

PUPIL As the teacher passes the ball to you, get off the mark and meet the ball. Using the inside of your right foot, pass the ball, directing it to just in front of the teacher's left foot, so that he can shoot if he wishes (fig. 87). This return pass shows how easily one of your team mates could score if your back is to the goal.

TEACHER Now tell the pupil to stand in front of the other goal post and repeat the exercise. This time the pupil will use his left foot to pass the ball back to you. You can then use your right foot to shoot at the goal. Only shoot if you want to: remember – you are the teacher!

Variations with the Return Ball

| TEACHER | Tell the pupil to stand in the centre of the goal area. Again, pass the ball to the pupil who should now meet the ball and play it back to you three separate ways: left of you, right of you, or straight back to you. Remember that you do not have to shoot.

Now swap positions (fig. 88) and choose which way to play the ball back to the pupil (fig. 89). As the pupil is about to strike, move out of the way to make it easier for him to score, as in fig. 90. With a return ball, the pupil must use his most convenient foot to shoot, regardless of where the ball comes from. The pupil will most likely strike the ball contrary to the rule in lesson 6 (page 48). This does not matter, so long as he strikes the ball correctly and scores goals.

Fig. 88 The centre of the goal is now used. Pupil passes to teacher.

Fig. 89 Teacher chooses which way to pass the ball back to pupil: left, right or straight back.

Fig. 90 Teacher decides to pass the ball straight back to pupil and gets out of the way. Pupil shoots at the goal.

PUPIL   You can practise first time passes anywhere on the pitch. Pass the ball back and forth to the teacher, using the inside of your foot. It is very important to practise using either foot – otherwise, how do you learn to use both feet equally well in a game?

Vary your positions; move from side to side or jog up and down the pitch together. Where possible, practise on a football pitch to get a feel for the space available in this whole area.

LESSON 15

ON THE PITCH

Playing a Ball Out of Defence
This next exercise will demonstrate safe play. During a game, a defender may need to play a long ball out of the danger area, or down the flanks. A long ball must only be used if there is not the option of a short pass.

TEACHER By now the pupil should be able to strike a ball reasonably well, using either foot. So executing a long and accurate pass will eventually come quite easily to him. However, depending on his age, the ball may not travel as far as he would like. This is not very important as he will be stronger when he is older.

Position the pupil close to the centre of the goal and stand on the right hand corner of the eighteen yard box. Now kick the ball firmly to the pupil, in the air or along the ground. The pupil should trap the ball ⇨ take it left out of the danger area (in the direction you are standing) ⇨ then strike the ball high towards you but over your head, using his left foot, as in fig. 91.

PUPIL You must quickly control the ball ⇨ look up and, at the same time, take the ball away from the centre of the goal ⇨ then deliver a long, high ball towards the teacher. Always approach the ball correctly and keep your eye on the ball when executing the strike. You do not need to run fast at the ball to gain power – your aim is to lift the ball and make it rise over the teacher's head.

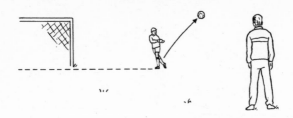

Fig. 91   Pupil takes the ball out of the danger area and strikes a high ball over teacher's head, using his left foot.

TEACHER Now stand on the left hand corner of the eighteen yard box which is on your left and repeat the exercise. The pupil should take the ball to his right hand side and use his right foot to strike the ball. Practise three times on the right hand side, three on the left hand side. After kicking the ball to the pupil you can move further away, the distance depending on his age. Tell the pupil to keep trying to lift the ball over your head.

Awareness in Midfield

TEACHER Position the pupil in the middle of the pitch, on the halfway line. Stand outside the circle and throw or kick the ball to him, as in fig. 92, then immediately jog in another direction. The pupil should control the ball then either strike or pass the ball back to you. Before you start the exercise tell the pupil:
1.   which foot to use to control the ball,
2.   whether to strike or pass back and which foot to use.
E.g. "Left foot control - right foot pass back" or "right foot control - right foot strike back".

The pupil should remain in the circle, but now you must vary the positions you throw or kick the ball from. Use at least four positions to allow the pupil to see the whole pitch and the different directions that he will face during a game.

PUPIL Control the ball and imagine that an opposing player is close by. Look up and quickly move the ball into a

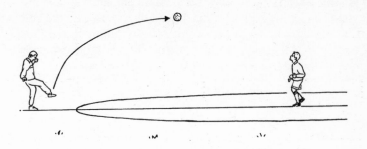

Fig. 92   Teacher kicks the ball to pupil, then jogs to another position.

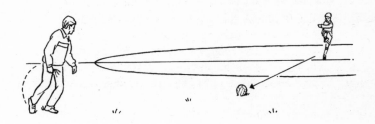

Fig. 93   Pupil controls the ball, then strikes it back to teacher.

good spot so you can execute a firm pass or strike accurately back to the teacher. Remember – it is easier for one of your own players to control the ball from a low, firm pass rather than one flying up in the air.

Corners

 PUPIL   You will now practise taking some corners while the teacher stands near the penalty spot. You will again strike your foot to the lower part of the ball and make it curl in. Strike the ball using the inner part of your boot near the lace holes. Take the corners from one side of the pitch, but strike the ball using alternate feet. The ball will either go slightly towards the goal or slightly away from the goal, depending on which foot you use (see figs. 94 and 95). If you have followed the course you should be able to take corners using either foot. Whether you do so in a game is another matter. This will depend on how much you perfect this, as well as your age and ability.

Fig. 94   **Right** foot curls ball **towards** goal.

Fig. 95   **Left** foot curls ball **away** from goal.

Now strike the ball using the centre of the lace area of your boot. Do you see the difference? While practising, remain on one side of the pitch and, if necessary, reduce the distance between you and the goal. Try to perfect your corners by making correct contact with the ball. Only stand a couple of metres behind the ball before you strike it. You do not need to take a long run up. When curling the ball, approach it more from the side.

Crossing the Ball

PUPIL   This is a similar action to that involved in taking corners, but this time you and the ball may be moving. This exercise is not a model for crossing the ball but, if practised well, it will provide you with plenty of scope for variation.

Ask the teacher to stand on the penalty spot – he is your target man. Move quickly with the ball, up and down the sideline. Turn at least three times, as in fig. 96a. You must keep the ball under control, but also keep your head up so that you can see the goal (fig. 96b). Now cross the ball, aiming for the target man.

Now repeat the exercise; but this time, just before you turn, pretend to kick the ball with either foot. This will serve three important purposes:

1.   to confuse your opponent
2.   to let you decide which foot to use and
3.   to give you time to pick the best moment to cross the ball.

This trick makes it easier for you to get the ball past your opponent and into the goal area (fig. 96c).

Now try two more variations on the cross:

● strike the ball using the centre of the lace area of your boot
● curl the ball using the method described in lesson 12, page 84.

With each, you will need to adjust your speed and turn your body accordingly. Use **alternate feet** to cross the ball and move gradually closer to the goal, depending on your age.

Fig. 96   a) Keeping your head up, move the ball quickly up and down the sideline, turning at least three times before you cross the ball.
b) Look at the goal and at the teacher.
c) This time, the cross goes in.

TEACHER It is important that the pupil learns how to cross the ball using either foot. Bringing the pupil closer to you will make it easier for him to do this and so will improve his confidence.

Final Lesson! Tap in Some Goals
Now we have reached the end of the lessons – WELL DONE! Both teacher and pupil deserve a big round of applause for working so hard (or not so hard, as the case may be!). For a bit of fun to celebrate your achievements, let's see if teacher and pupil can score some easy goals.

Fig. 97 Pupil passes ball from the left so teacher taps in the goals with his left foot.

PUPIL Position yourself as in fig. 97. Pass an accurate ball across the face of the goal, so the teacher can (try to) score some goals. Pass the ball from either side of the goal using your right foot, then your left foot, and so on. Strike the ball, and use a side foot pass. Ask the teacher to try and tap the ball in using the inside of his foot. When you pass the ball from the right, the teacher should use his right foot to tap in the goals, and vice versa.

Fig. 98   Now swap positions – teacher passes ball from the right so pupil taps in the goals with his right foot.

> **TEACHER**   Now swap positions and pass the ball from either side of the pupil, as in fig. 98. The pupil should then tap the ball into the goal using the inside of either foot.

To make it a bit more tricky, use a smaller goal, a set target, or even a goalkeeper. However you do it, both of you should keep your eyes on the ball, and do not miss!

ALL ROUND VARIATIONS

| PUPIL | This next section lists a number of points you can refer to, but, as your ability increases, most of these will become second nature to you.

Passing or Striking the Ball
Place one foot alongside the ball and keep your eye on the ball.

- *To increase height*, strike your foot to the **lower** part of the ball, close to the ground.
- *To keep the ball low*, strike your foot to the **middle** or **upper** part of the ball.
- *To curl a ball inwards*, use the area between the lace area and the **inside** of your boot to strike the ball.
- *To curl a ball outwards*, use the area between the lace area and the **outside** of your boot to strike the ball.
- *To increase power*, **speed up** your foot movement, then follow through, striking the ball accurately.
- *To increase the effect*, **accentuate** the body action and use more physical effort.

Controlling the Ball
Keep your eye on the ball, judge the speed the ball is travelling and then cushion the bounce.

- *To control the ball with your feet*, use the **side** of your foot where possible.
- *To control a high ball with your chest*, **lean back** and cushion the ball with your chest.

- *To control a lower ball with your chest,* **lean forwards**, arch your shoulders in and direct the ball to the ground.

Heading the Ball
Keep your eyes open and direct the ball where you want it to go with your forehead. Your forehead should end up facing the same direction as the ball is travelling.

- *To head a fast moving ball,* meet it with **full forehead contact**.
- *To head a slow moving ball,* arch your back, bring your **neck back** and **attack the ball**.
- *To make a glancing header,* make **slight forehead contact** with the ball.

THE FINAL PART

PRACTICE

PUPIL We now arrive at the last section of the book, but, before we continue, let me remind you to **keep practising all of the lessons**. Go over any areas where you feel there is a weakness. It is quite usual for a player to kick the ball with his best foot, or to rely on his strengths in a game. But if you have any weaknesses these will always show. Choose from all the lessons and use a good variety of exercises each time you practise. This should help you to learn more quickly and it will make it more interesting.

The first part of this section will give some advice to the very young and to those of you who have not yet started playing for a team. Do not rush into playing for a team: consider how proficient you could become if you practise your skills for just two hours each week. This would give you loads of ball possession in a year; in a game you only get about three minutes.

Why Practise?
Most players will need about three months' regular practice to see a real improvement in their skills, or even longer if they are playing for a team. Remember: if you are lacking the skills in practice, how are you going to cope at a faster pace when playing in a team?

What Position?
If you have practised over several months, you should be fairly confident of playing in any position on the pitch. The more skill you have acquired the more adaptable you will be.

You could end up playing in only one position, although I feel that this is not a good idea. Nonetheless, you will, at some point, find the position which suits you best.

Limit Your Speed
It is very important not to rush your play. Take your time and use the skills that you have learnt. Limit the use of your speed when in possession of the ball and try, when possible, to keep hold of the ball. This is not a suggestion that you slouch around the football pitch, or that you hog the ball, but merely of a way to avoid making mistakes while at the same time improving your confidence on the ball.

Hold on to the Ball
If you hold the ball up and do not always run forward with the ball, you will become more aware of the other players around you. As you become older and gain more experience, you will know where to play the ball even before you receive it. More passing options will become available to you, your speed will increase on the pitch and will be used more often (with sensible restraint, though). This will be a natural progression as you grow and as you play more games.

The Wrong Time
We often see older teenage players who have skill but fail to impress on the pitch. Often their eagerness causes them to make blatant mistakes. This can occur when poor teamplay or being rushed forces them into bad habits. An example of this is the youngster who just happens to be a fast runner. He can use his speed in preference to skill which sometimes looks impressive. However, he has probably learnt to use his speed at the wrong time and so neglected his technique. This just may prove to be his downfall.

Lacking Speed
A player may be skilful throughout his childhood but, when he gets older, find that he lacks speed. We should never presume that everything will work out just as we hope. However, it is far better to take your time when you are young than to rush

your play and so become susceptible to bad habits. A player will always shine by using skill as his main asset.

THE LEVELS OF FOOTBALL

Young Success
A child of eight or nine has a long way to go before he reaches adult level football. Some youngsters may be noticed by national football clubs. This is no guarantee of success, but it's nonetheless encouraging.

Will I Get Noticed?
Youngsters between twelve and sixteen have a good opportunity to show their ability. Schools will put forward players to represent their town or county. Clubs will nominate players to represent leagues. This, together with playing in a good team or reaching a cup final, may lead to some recognition. However; there is no set route to success. Opportunities may come and go in football but there are other ways to get recognised and progress. Throughout the country there are different levels of football, from the lower adult ranks through to national leagues. Many a player has come from the lower ranks and made it to top class football. Therefore, to play at local senior level may prove to be a good start for any youngster.

How to Play when you are Older
Watch the top players in action, whether live or on TV, and you will see that they are agile, accurate, quick and they make the game look easy. Well, playing the game *is* easy to them. The only trial they face is a training session between matches. So, if you are sixteen or older, what should you be doing? Copying the best player you know of and following his pattern of play.

The Test
If you learn to play football steadily at first, you will progress over the years and use more speed, more so when really put to the test. All players will face a test when they try to reach a

higher level of football. You will need to prove that you are capable of fitting in with the team, first by showing adequate skill and composure, then by speeding up your pace. Each level is that much harder to reach than the last, yet your skill and composure will remain the real test. If you are also quick and agile you may go higher – even to the top!

The Way to Play

Observe any boys' match and see if you can spot the best player in that team. If you are not sure, ask their manager. Observe what this player does in the game. I am sure you will recognise how he reacts on the ball. He will be agile yet stay firmly on the ball. He will keep his poise, move in any direction and show confidence with only short bursts of speed. He will not chase around needlessly.

Save Your Energy

Many younger boys' football matches are quite physical, yet often lacking in skill. Depending on the quality of the team, you will need to adjust to this and, to some extent, play your own game. This is not to say that you must pussyfoot around, but only use your strength when you need to.

THE IMPORTANCE OF GOOD TEACHING

TEACHER   The **way** the pupil is taught is just as important as **what** he is taught, so it is vital that you get it right at this early stage in your youngster's learning. Here are some points to consider.

Ball Contact

Correct ball contact is a vital skill so should be the first thing to learn. In football, as in all ball sports, making a good contact with the ball comes with experience. However, compared to a golf ball or a tennis ball, a football is quite large, so this should make it easier to strike it accurately. The biggest problem can occur when the ball is travelling fast and low towards the player – this really puts his judgment to the test.

Striking a fast moving ball low and accurately is not easy, but if he is going to shoot in this situation, it is preferable to miss the target wide than to sweep the ball high into the air. The pupil should practise low shots and direct the ball so it travels close to the ground. The important points to remember are for him to:

- keep his eye on the ball
- strike the ball correctly.

Accuracy

A player's accuracy on the pitch is fundamental to his and his team's performance. There is no point in shooting, heading or passing the ball unless it goes exactly in the direction that it is supposed to. All players make mistakes on the pitch, but when practising there is no need to rush. This also applies in warm up, or when just tapping the ball between two or three players. The pupil needs to perfect his aim and learn to slow his pace.

Increasing the Pupil's Awareness

A player must learn to keep his head up and look around him. If he keeps his eye fixed only on the ball, another player may then nip in and take it away from him. This could happen if the ball is coming towards him, or even just as he receives it. A player should only look at the ball as it nears him. It only takes a short time to pass or control a ball, but he needs a long look to see who's around . . .

Keep it Simple

There is no need for youngsters to exert too strenuous an effort. Most young players will gain more from practising simple skills such as quick ball control, agile movements and tapping the ball about, than from gruelling sessions of repeating long kicks.

Changes that Occur

When playing a game of football, changes will occur in the way a player executes a skill. Such changes are governed by several factors:

- the speed of a pass
- the condition of the pitch
- how much time the player has on the ball
- the player's own peculiarities and so on.

Players will change their technique to suit a situation, so set patterns are bound to be disrupted during the course of a game, regardless of how they have been executed in practice.

Motivation

When a child is enjoying being taught, he learns more. His interest will be maintained if you vary the sequence of his exercises. As he progresses, praise him and explain the reason for the praise. Watch his performance closely and do not scold him if he makes a mistake: instead, suggest a way in which to correct the error. At times you will need to compromise, especially when things are not going quite as well as they should be. Be prepared to pause the practice if he is becoming distracted or irritable. Let the child do something different with the ball, or allow him to choose what he wants to do (within reason!).

Feedback

Using the one-to-one teaching method will make it easier for the pupil to improve his performance. Look for any exercises that may seem difficult, then, if you feel you are up to it, demonstrate the sequence to the pupil – but be careful to get it right! Alternatively, watch a professional football match and point out the skills that the pupil needs to practise. When he performs a technique correctly, ask him to describe how the action felt so that he develops an understanding for the correct movement and will be able to repeat it.

Fitness and Fatigue

Most children are reasonably fit, so they should be able to perform a suitable amount of ball work without becoming too tired. However, putting on too much of a strain will not increase a youngster's skill. Therefore, do not increase a child's physical work until he shows good progress in his skills.

The Way we are Built
Players vary in all shapes and sizes: tall, short, thin or stocky. But size doesn't matter. All footballers need to be very fit and have a high level of stamina, but even this will vary from one player to the next. Youngsters are all different and all will show strengths in a variety of ways. Do not attempt to anticipate a child's development or chances of success from his present build or stature.

Expectations
We all set up expectations at one time or another, but these can prove damaging; not only to a teacher, but also a child. It is easy to think only of success, but a youngster will get on better without feeling the need to succeed. There will be proud moments, when a child does progress, and disappointment if he fails. However, 'pushiness' and impatience will not improve a child's ability or performance. All a teacher can do is encourage, support and praise the child, hoping that he will try to do the best that he possibly can.

A "Grown Up's" Influence
The influence that a parent, tutor, or other guiding 'grown up' has over a child may be greater than you think. Now and again, one sees parents of very young children shouting aggressive abuse from the touchline. Children often react to this aggression by running faster, making more mistakes, tackling badly, or even causing fouls. Adults **must** learn to keep their emotions under control. This behaviour will never help a child to progress and may even spoil his chances.

To call out "well done – great pass!" or "great shot!" or "never mind, get your head up!" shows a far more positive attitude. Your enthusiasm should encourage *good play*, rather than winning.

Other ways to influence a child beneficially are to tell him to "keep your head up", "take your time", "control the ball" or "don't rush your pass" and so on. You must stay calm throughout the game and let the youngster get on with it. Brief and basic advice is enough, given just before the game or perhaps at half time.

THE GAME TO PRACTISE

| TEACHER | How do we make a youngster more aware of what's going on around him in a game? How do we increase his confidence and encourage him to pass more? The answer: restrict the player going forward on the ball and limit tackles in a game.

Young players have an urge to go forward, especially when they shouldn't. This is evident when a player runs headlong into trouble, or when he misses a good opportunity to pass. Holding up the play will make youngsters more aware of the other players around them. This will create more back up play and passing around the team, instead of their team mates scattering in all directions.

The following game is designed purely to help increase players' levels of awareness by holding up play in an exaggerated way. You can play the game with any even number of players between four and twenty. Use a pitch of size relative to the number of players.

The game is played just like any other game, with the following extra rules:

1. The player who has possession of the ball **cannot go forward with the ball**. He may take the ball sideways, backwards or pass the ball in any direction, but he must not run or even walk forward more than one or two steps with the ball.

2. When a player has possession of the ball, all opposing players **must stay a distance of one metre away** and **not tackle**. Any loose balls will go in the opposition's favour, more so if there is a dispute. Any 50-50 balls will go in favour of the first player to put his foot on top of the ball. The opposing player must then back off the one metre distance.

3. No long shots are allowed. If you have a total of four players in the game, a player must be within two metres of the goal before he can shoot. If you have a total of six players in the game, a player must be within three metres of the goal to shoot. Increase the shooting distance by one metre for each additional two players. Therefore,

with twenty players the shots at goal will be no further than ten metres away.

4.   Free kicks will be awarded against any player not adhering to these rules. All other football rules will apply as normal.

Use these rules at each training session before your normal game. See how the players' confidence grows and how the team play improves over a period of time.

POSITIONS ON THE PITCH

PUPIL Now for some good advice for players on three separate areas of the pitch: forward, midfield and defence. Try to remember this advice on the pitch, even though things may not always go to plan.

THE FORWARD POSITION
(Attacker and Striker)

In a game, there are usually two strikers who play up front in the team. Both will have a better opportunity to score goals than the rest of the team. Both strikers will need to combine with the midfield players who support them.

As a striker, you will often have your back to the opposition when you receive the ball. **Move away from your defender** and into a good position so that your team mates can play the ball **along the ground** to you. If you receive the ball in this manner and you are not sure what to do, **shield the ball**, **keep it at your feet**, but **look up**; only then can you decide your best option.

When you are going forward with the ball, try to keep the ball **close to your feet**. This will make the defender uncertain when to tackle. Keeping your **head up** will give you the confidence to vary your play and a quick burst of **speed** will put the defender behind you. Turn and move the ball into a space; this will give you more time to consider what to do next.

When you are going forward without a defender, this is a good time to use your speed. You could push the ball well forward, then run, but **steady yourself** as you approach the goalkeeper. Keep your **eye on the goal** then decide what to do: either shoot or go round him.

If you are close to or in the penalty area with the ball, try a shot. If you are in same position without the ball, **move from space to space**. You must try to gain possession of the ball to stay in the game or score.

The best way for your team to go forward and still keep possession of the ball is by using **short**, **accurate passes**. So use one of your team mates to pass to and then position yourself for the return ball.

If you are a striker, you will need to score goals with your head, so your **timing** and **forehead contact** are vital. You must also learn to defend, so close down the opposition, limit their space and chase.

When you do not have the ball, **do not run away** from your team mates. Do not expect them to pass a long ball to you over the defender's head unless, of course, you are certain of reaching it. Remember: a good defender will most likely win a 50-50 ball.

Scoring plenty of goals does not necessarily mean you are a brilliant player. If you are good at playing up front, move into midfield, or even defence, to gain more experience.

MIDFIELD

Usually, there are four players in midfield, but adult or more experienced teams often play with five. The midfield players will be in and around the centre of the pitch, but they also cover the left and right side (also known as the 'flanks'). During a game, these players will often support both the defence and attack. Other times they will be winning the ball in the midfield or masterminding forward play. Therefore, if you want to play midfield, you will have to be adaptable.

Most teams will have two types of midfield players: the ones who are clever on the ball and the ones who are stronger at tackling. A midfield player's first priority is to help the defence, especially in the first fifteen minutes of a game. This is the time to assess the opposition and make your presence felt in the game. Look to help your defenders, call to receive the ball, or get into a space.

If you are near to an opposing player who has the ball, move and limit his space. Hold your ground and, if he runs, go with him, force a mistake and chase. If you are a long way away from an opposing player who has the ball, pick up and mark another player. Always think defensively: you may need to chase him.

During a game, the ball will go back and forth many times, most likely in the air (especially in boys' games). Because of this, you must slow down – or even walk. Pace yourself for when you need to run. This will help to calm you down and allow you to see any mistakes. Remember: **slow your pace, this is not a race!**

If your team has possession of the ball, get into a space and then call. If you receive the ball, quickly control the ball, look up, then decide the best option to take. Remember that when you have the ball there is no need to beat your opposite players: moving quickly into a space and passing could prove to be the best option to take.

Do not attempt to beat an opponent in your own half of the pitch, or near the halfway line, unless you have clearly wrong-footed the opponent. Always remember that possession of the ball is your top priority. Most youngsters play the ball up and down the pitch, but you must look to play the ball sideways. There will be players in space for this type of ball so look out for them.

Have you ever played in a five a side game? The pitch is a lot smaller and you need to be nimble. Well, be nimble when you are close to your opponents' penalty area. This will give you the time to hold the ball or make short passes, without any danger to your own team. Make this your practice area to gain in confidence on the ball.

If possible, play in all of the midfield positions, then try attack and defence.

DEFENCE

There are normally four defenders in a side, but some older or more experienced teams play with just three. The basic function of a defender is to stop the opposition reaching the goal and scoring; how they do this is another matter. Vision, speed and timing all play an important role. Good defenders will also be skilful at passing accurate balls, going forward, and supporting the attack. So, if you want to be a defender, don't think that you've just got to be a 'stopper': remember that you will need to defend when the opposition has the ball, so don't give the ball away!

There are often two types of defender: the tall type and the fast type. If you have both of these assets, then defence may well prove to be your speciality.

Although goal-keepers haven't previously been mentioned in this book, defenders must have a good understanding of them. You must know what they are doing, why they are doing it and when they will do it. Keep an eye on a professional goalie and get to know how he plays.

As a general rule, intercepting the ball must be your first option. Whether the ball is in the air or on the ground, if you can get to it first, do so. Try to anticipate a pass or a move and this will give you a good advantage over the opposition.

Push your team forward when they have possession of the ball, but make sure there is still cover at the back. Get a good idea of the ability of the opposition early in the game, especially the player whom you may need to mark.

As a defender, you will see the ball come towards you very often. This is an advantage, so make the most of it. Keep your eye on the ball and then decide your action. If you are going to mark a player, then stay tightly with him, but do not tackle from behind. Be sure to keep your eye on the ball.

If an opposing player is coming towards you with the ball, move to one side and show him which way you want him to go. Try to always force him away from the goal, but stay on your feet and, if you tackle, make it a good one – firm and towards the ball. Always remember that any tackle must be sensible and that you must make contact with the ball only – this way players will not get hurt and you will not be penalised.

If the ball comes to you in your own penalty area, just remember that, **if in doubt, put the ball out**. This type of play may not look very skilful, but may nevertheless prove important. And, of course, be extra careful with your tackles in the penalty area.

Always look to support your team and call for the ball if you are in space. Always try to cover one of your players if he is going in for a tackle. Stay behind him so that, if he loses the ball, you are next in line to stop the opposition coming through.

As a defender, it is still important to show your talent on the ball. This position may, however, limit your time on the ball and cause you to rush your play on a number of occasions. You may not have the opportunity to experiment or go forward as much as you would like. As a young player, you need a great deal of ball possession in order to gain experience. So, switch your position and play several games in midfield or attack throughout the season.

AN IMPORTANT NOTE

For all attack minded players create space, find space and get into space.

THE LAST WORD

PUPIL & TEACHER As you will know by now, learning, or teaching, football skills is hard work. If you both keep at it, you should see that it is also very rewarding. Whether you reach the World Cup or the local park, if you are committed enough and if you try hard enough, your well-practised football skills will allow you to shine above the rest.

INDEX

To order these Right Way titles please fill in the form below

No. of copies	Title	Price	Total
	Begin Fishing the Right Way	£4.99	
	Freshwater Fishing Properly Explained	£4.99	
	The Right Way to Read Music	£5.99	
	For P&P add £2.50 for the first book, £1 for each additional book		
	Grand Total		£

Name: _____

Address: _____

_____ Postcode: _____

Daytime Tel. No./Email: _____

Three ways to pay:

1. Telephone the TBS order line on **01206 255 800**.
   Order lines are open Monday – Friday, 8:30am – 5:30pm.

2. I enclose a cheque made payable to **TBS Ltd** for _____

3. Please charge my ☐ Visa   ☐ Mastercard   ☐ Amex   ☐ Maestro

   Card number: _____

   Expiry date:_____ (Maestro issue no._____)

   Signature: _____
   (your signature is essential when paying by debit or credit card)

Please return forms to Cash Sales/Direct Mail Dept., The Book Service, Colchester Road, Frating Green, Colchester CO7 7DW.

Enquiries to readers@constablerobinson.com.

Constable and Robinson Ltd (directly or via its agents) may mail, email or phone you about promotions or products.

☐ Tick box if you do not want these from us   ☐ or our subsidiaries.

www.right-way.co.uk
www.constablerobinson.com